I0422167

An Ink Fruit

Streets
(VOLUME I)

Hari Das

Table of Content

Forward

Streets a place where people exceed their strength when the day starts, from nil to crowded and then the same phenomena with an opposite effect happen to end a day, from crowded to nil. In between this rate of fluctuation of public I had seen and calculated some fact and figures by taking a close look over these coming and going crowd. I was able to do this because what I believe is whenever I drop my footsteps over these streets my soul gets automatically connected to the world and nature and then this energy sourcing earth tells me where I have to go and at that time I can't resist myself then on the streets I flow like a gentle breeze and pass by the people and crowd as unknown. Maximum time my travels on the streets are attempts to find something somewhere in some part of the street that I believe it waits for me to get caught. I feel exhausted but then also I walk because my instinct doesn't allow me to leave the path I follow. This curiosity to know or to get that I follow by listening to my heart and as a result at the end of the day I never come back empty handed. And at last when it is there in front of my eyes then it makes me feel sufficient to calculate its existence in this breath taking life. People come over here for short time may be just to pass but some people come over here for never going back. They stay here like numbness hiding in certain corners of the streets and sometimes I am one of them.

Hari Das

Lake-1

My vision continued to trace an end of a lake, from window side I was traveling in a bus towards Bhopal, the capital city of Madhya Pradesh one of the Indian state situated in the central part of India. It was morning at 6; the weather was little bit cold. Here in the central part of India it was almost an end to the winter season. My bus was crossing an over bridge of Bhopal lake during that time surprisingly I had seen a splendid effect of nature there over the lake water yes and I was awed. The rising sun dropped its first warm yellow graces over the cool lake water by lifting the light white fog coated over the lake. The tiny moving blue waves with a pace of moving wind shimmered its sleeves and leaved a glassy shine in my eyes. My Twitching eyes reflected a vision towards my father and I remembered what he said when I was just leaving my home for Bhopal "A City of Lake's you are going to visit my boy, don't lose yourself with those magnificent effect of nature, I know you are a wandering fellow but you should remember your purpose of visit dear I hope you will best off luck". Yes he was right those blue tiny waves were trying me to take me away in a land of fascination where I was sitting there in lake side dreaming about her; there I halted my mind to stop visualizing further for keeping those words as orders delivered by my father. The lake was surrounded with average heightened hills, but the end of the lake was still not visible because of removing white fogs leaded me to think how endless is this lake a big watery lake and yes it was.

In that lake a fisher man was throwing his net from a small boat to catch fresh water fishes. My mouth watered by thinking the taste of those fishes if it had arrived in a well garnished plate. Then as soon as the bus crossed the bridge the city welcomed us with a two lane road bounded with rocky slopes of crest and troughs in both the sides following as waves with the motion of bus. Where alongside the passing wide footpaths as well in the divider too there where neatly shaped plants of freshly bloomed yellow flowers they were dangling their heads with the pass of wind and were ready to be plucked. The greenery continued in all square slops and curves. Finally it ended when the bus entered in a densely populated area to reach the final stop as a fool stop at the bus stand.

This populated area was quiet inverse from rest of the outer part of the city from where I traveled that was full of uneven elevations and somewhat isolated. But here it was full of dust with heavy flow of morning traffic, horning and moving sound of vehicles; under construction roads it just felt like the city had woken up earlier for an important work to be done for the day. A real Indian city likewise mine so it was not new to me, where small houses apartments and shops were stick to each other without giving a single inches of gap hence no sign of greenery anywhere . There in the road sides people were roaming here and there recklessly crossing the streets, passing by footpaths going to office with a raised temper in tension, shop keepers opening their shops, children going to school in a jolly mood with their tightly pinched water bottle resting on their chest hooked up from the neck with their mamas holding their fingers, few ladies buying vegetables from a hawker by blushing out the real market price of vegetables in high pitch that they know very well for bargaining. A homeless man was laying at the edges of a footpath behaving as calm and cool by angling his legs and crossing his arms beneath the head as a rest was thinking wide with his long hairs touching the wide footpaths may be about his past how it passed with lots of ups and downs he faced. But somewhat it seemed he is planned with some kind of idea that he will follow to get some money for his next eat. Like this many other things and happenings passed away from my window side by giving brief ideas of the things happening around in a flow of bus.

Finally the bus entered in the bus stop by giving several jerks caused by the speed breakers. Leaving their seats passengers lined up where I was in mid of the row. As soon as I stepped out men in green shirts, the auto drivers were all ready present at the gate asking the passengers about their destination in the city. As their usual habit the auto drivers were giving mutually a tough look in a fit of rage towards each other to take away the passengers. Where one of them asked me where you have to go but I know these auto drivers very well how they treat these new arrivals in the city, by fooling the public in a way by charging huge amount for even a kilometer. So I just removed myself from them, though I dint had any intention to hire auto as well. I started walking further rolling my huge bag consisting of large amount of study materials and a little amount of clothes as the stay was only for ten days for my PG exams centered this time in Bhopal. Here then onwards my first intention was to get a cheap lodge near by the bus stand, to feel easy for further travels in the city. So I took a safe corner in a cigarette shop at the entry side of the bus stop to ask someone. I lighted a cigarette, and after having few puffs I asked that cigarette vendor called paanwala in India because they also provide paan(A special kind of preparation combining betel leaf with areca nut with some sweet ingredient and tobacco) to chew. Can u please tell me where I can get a cheap lodge? He dint heard me at first as his speeding hands showed how busy he was in making paans for his customers who were waiting. But then I asked again, this time he heard and within a second he replied some name it was not clear to my ears and I felt totally confused what he said? What was it? I was screwed. Now this time I was feeling awkward to ask one more time as I can act as a disturbing element for him in this peak time of his business. But then I thought I think I should not waste my time. Anyhow he is not going to kill me for asking a silly question. Then I dint went to think much. As a shameless I asked it again what you said can you please repeat it again. This time the vendor irrelatively by biting his teeth in his enraged voice he said "imily gali" by pointing his hands towards a narrow street going inside from the main road. For a second I was literally frightened the kind of facial expression he gave it to me. Somehow it was expected from him so it was fine for me. In hurry I said ok and by giving thanks I took two more long puffs of my cigarette, thrown it away and moved on. There in front of me a busy main road was there where big rolling tiers of buses and trucks with heavy vroom sound, honing cars and scooters passed by me in left and right direction.

Soon the road cleared off and I crossed the main road by rolling my bags. After crossing I straightly walked into the narrow street pointed by the cigarette vendor. There I had seen the street was full of shops at both the sides. A deep glance I made over the boards of shops in both the sides it was written mobile shops, with different names of vendors. There I understood I am there in a mobile market then it means I need to get into this street a bit more for imily gali. After a brief walk the mobile market was over and I was there in a small square. But I dint turned anywhere from that square also I went straight and entered in another narrow street where I had seen a market of lodges same as mobile market and this was imily gali. Here where ever my eyes went huge boards of color blue, white, red and many other of rectangular cubical shape in which name of the lodges were written but vertically hooked in each three to four storied buildings of this street. After reading these boards I felt saved and relaxed as I got the place without spending lot of time and effort. Now it was time to select a good lodge. Fortunately I got one. I went into navya lodge with again a brief walk into the street. As it was good looking newly constructed three storied building well painted, dark varnished windows and doors, with a big balcony my favorite spot in the world. But in comparison to this lodge others were old with cracks on their walls unpainted and with a small balcony same look as Mumbai red street buildings which I dint liked.

By a constant negotiation I took a room of double bed, but no TV for 200 rupees per day that was cheap. No TV was a disappointment but later it went as fruit full to me. I got a balcony side room in second floor. The lodge had same arrangement like hospitals so many rooms adjacent to each other in both the sides divided by a big corridor that at the end was giving a round staircase towards down floor and in front it was balcony. So finally I was there in my room. For a while on exploring I found, my room was having two beds covered with clean white bed sheets attached to each other pulled up in one corner. In front of it a hair dressing table with mirror attached and a small table was kept aside. Over this table a glass with water jug was kept that I dint even went to use as I had seen the dirty stains over the edges of both. At last my sight ended with bathroom, attached in one corner of the room but I dint went for a look thinking that it should be clean. By the time it was 8 in the morning but due to long travel I was feeling sleepy. Although the distance towards Bhopal from my city is just of four hours so it can't be even said as long but you know the Indian roads it will never let you sleep. There I jumped by leaving my whole weight over my fluffy bed and closed my eyes for a sleep. Seconds passed, minutes passed but I was not able to sleep because the things of those manipulating streets that I had seen were coming in my thoughts again and again as I am still there in travel. Twisting sometimes left sometimes right I was totally fed up of my wandering mind. At last after struggling hard anyhow I was caught up with sleep.

There after darkness prevailed in my eyes as night took me to a ride. Very soon intense of my sleep took me to a depth went inside darkness tied, loosed my grip from my body shell. There soul inside flushed outside, fell into a gorge as a water fall. Crashed into a river where dreams flowing inside, as streamlined fishes directed one side. Flow of river offered a dream and took me away with its bulgy streams. Soon the dreams I got, rushed from the brain reached in my eyes and shown me a vision of that lake site. There at the lake side concrete steps I was sitting with a seeking eyes in search of a girl called My Lady "a belonging from my past" from that infinity of Fogy Lake, which uttered nothing other than dismay. Her absence in life immerged out in me as roly poly sorrow full tears, which tapped the gentle flow of lake, and formed some elusive circles in the Lake water site. And their again after a long time she came into me as a sunflower bloomed with the first tap of sunlight, where her lovely fascinating adorable face was visible in the lake water as a beauteous dream resting in the cool water site. Rising sun dazzled her face. Her curly hair curves in waves breezing wind flowing waves. There her eyes in dark water illuminated my weeps in lake water. Her eyes her lips her nose her face was calling me, in desperate to touch her there in the deep lake water. But the touch I made the sleeves of waves took her away went away to never come back in my ways. I remember the last glance we made My Lady. Your well-formed eyes I know what it spelled to my indigent eyes, I want to cry in your chest if you will give me for a while. Through my eyes my mind told to her eyes a mistake I did, it count be corrected anyway back, though I have to leave. Now even my shade also, will not be there around you anymore, to follow you in your any part of life and then you don't have to restrict your legs to move around My Lady yes my dear. But I needed you for my whole life that you can't give me in this span of sight. Even though I am feeling glad towards my fate, as I was able to be a stain of that moon who can never forget the darkness hiding behind that tantalizing yen. You as a flower I loosed My Lady, sometimes I think. There nostalgic fever captures my ink. To pass this trauma it takes time to sink though I have to manage myself. Yes I do with your fresh morning fragments that I still hail in me, somewhere as those breath taking arguments we did. I know my dear you love me but you are bounded with limitations that I respect. So without any hesitation I am letting you free from this curse of love. Live your own life; be happy, get married have kids but remember one thing, I will wait for you, yes My Lady, somewhere one day after the end of that darkness when you will close your eyes to never get opened. I will get you there in form of light. My hands will be there for you to raise your soul from your body pod that was always mud for me, my light. I will pray to my soul thereafter if there is any life we will live together as a pair of humming bird flying towards the eastern sunrise.

Hari Das

Lake

Wind in pace
Water with laze
Moved its self
Waves

I hailed down my fumes
Deep down it roomed
A face
A shape
Crystal and clear
In Lake

Surface of water
Her face
In Black water

Surface of water
Brown eyes
Deep there in water

Surface of water
Water
your face
Face
I still remember,
There in lake water

Moved my palms
To touch the water
Water
Gentle and lentil
No harm in water

Broken dreams
Took a shape
Fluctuating water
Colored lake
Lake
Lake

Waves took her away
As sleeves of past
Went to a way
To never come back

Her face
My ways
Took unknown shape
Unknown race
Swept away
With some sleeves of lake
Some sleeves of lake
Sleeves of lake
Lake....

Poetry is music a rhythm so read it lovely and smoothly

Hari Das

Captured-2

Somehow my sleep went off I woke up and leaned against the wall. In this half asleep state, I stared everywhere in my room but me and my loneliness only I could find. She again came into my dreams, as a resemblance of my divine past, when I was with her. There sadness began to capture my heart in an extreme need of her and it was irresistible for me. There in a sudden Impatient state I jerked my head to remove her from my thoughts else I know, I will be spoiling my whole day in an agony without studying for my exams. But the jerk dint worked. My cozy heart in her absence as a wound began to feel the silence of my room. Very soon the numbness hiding in my room brake's its silence, by removing her from my thoughts my puzzled head heard an up roaring babbling sound of so many happenings outside. And I was shore it is from the streets downside.

In the morning time when I entered in this lodge it was a vacant street. So in a curiosity to know this hush Kush atmosphere I went into the balcony leaving my room opened. There I lighted a cigarette and rested my hands over the wide railing of my balcony. Releasing my fumes the flow of wind was towards east and it was already noon I realized from the heat. From there my first sight from the balcony I made. Literally if I would say, I was amazed, that much that if a little bit of feeling left for her in me, in a mean time it was also root upped, on viewing such a breathing crowded street, which was giving a feel of liveliness made me feel fresh and colorful in sight. A real view of crowded street of Bhopal I was able to see from this second floor of my lodge. Each and every think happening on the streets was crystal and clear to my cupid eyes. So many pedestrians were coming and going from where? Somewhere like a current flow of two rivers like mixed against each other who were struggling hard to cross each other. A peep I directly made straight toward downside of my lodge by raising my ankles at tip toe to overcome the height of the railing but nothing was visible at the ground floor in my side. As the aluminum sheets were coming out, which were acting as a shade for the shop and shop owners for their customers. In my whole lane the condition was same. Fortunately the shop's in opposite lane with the rabble street was clearly visible. Beside each lodge in both the lane at the ground floor was occupied by these shop owners selling daily household and other personal utility items that were acting as the major attraction for the public towards this street.

A small tea vendor I had seen in front of my lodge with his single iron bench that he was using as a tea stall. He was preparing tea for his customers but no place to sit that was acting as a big trouble for the customer's arriving. So the people were resting their bumps in certain nooks and corners if found suitable to keep and were having tea in a relaxing state, near to the tea stall. There I had seen a group of young men's laughing wide don't know why, may be through some joke shared. There after continuing their conversation they were having there sip of tea and smoke in one side. Near to them two old men's of bolt head with sleeves on their forehead felt tensed. They were having a serious talk in a manner they were trying to sort out some serious issue. As an acceptance of understanding both of them were nodding their head towards each other like two cuckoo birds sitting aside. Soon there glasses became empty with no sips left they paid and went off.

Thereafter from in between the crowd, I had seen a traditional Indian joint family arriving from the left hand side of the street. The women's in that family were showered in colorful Indian traditional attire. The bright full colored printed sarees they wore, red bindi stuck on their foreheads, a golden mangalsutra(A chain wore by Indian ladies if they are married as a sign)hanging in their necks, silver and gold rings and earrings, jingling glass bangles filled in their hands, huge makeup in their silky faces. Each and everything about these women's from this floor, my eyes felt like they as a beautiful jewelry is worn by this street. In that family a teenage girl with his small brother in there western outfits were walking recklessly by giving a deep glance over the street side shops. It was clearly visible a big question was lingering in their faces. What to buy? By giving the leadership to their family the men's in their Europium shirt pant outfits were walking forward by holding hands of their small children, where the gossiping women's were coming after them. Soon after few steps the families get distributed as they were already planned.

From them two women's with an old lady might be their mother in law entered in a jewelry shop who's shiny reflection was twinkling in my eyes from the glass door of that jewelry shop, a couple entered in a bangle shop adjacent to it, that teenage girl with his small brother entered in a cosmetic shop adjacent to the bangle shop and at last husband's of those three women's who entered in jeweler shop walked a while a little leaving two three shops with the small children of that family and entered in a photo frame shop. There I had seen the shop keeper of that photo frame shop gives them a warm welcome with a sweet smile embedded in his face, might be thinking that he got a good art loving client. Now these three men's in which an old man and two young men's probably his sons began to give a deep glace over the beautiful paintings and sceneries hooked up in the photo frame shop. Where the shop keeper was standing beside them crossing his palms in how may I help you mode. Then suddenly what happent the old men enthusiastically called his two sons to join him to understand a meaning full painting that he got. There all the three men's began to stare on that painting with their wide eyes opened to understand the flow of that art but I was not able to see from here is because they were standing in front of it. In other hand the shop keeper smile widened joyfully with his teeth shining, thinking that I am just going to sell out one of my painting. Waving his hand the old man called the shop keeper also and said to explain this painting as an order. As soon as he screwed his eyes on the painting and went for the first word to utter there was a call from one of the lady from the street side who came back from the jewelry shop. Not bothering about the shop keeper and his painting in a quick zeal all of them led the spot without collecting any response. A sudden loss of anticipation reflected in his face. There from behind, the shop keeper raised his hands to call them back but released by scribbling some ugly words his lip movement told. The entire family member reunited at the same spot, where they get distributed carrying small covers and packets they bought. Then by giving a walk the women's seemed sharing the details of the purchase they made. The family went off with a seeking eye for the next purchase to be made. After they went my eyes became impatient, to know what was exactly there in that painting and why dint they bought. I turned and focused my eyes on that painting hooked up between other major paintings of Mona Lisa, The Last Supper, Starry Nights, Pablo Picasso and others. And when I got the view I chuckled delightfully. Finally I understood it was just a time pass for them because it was just a silly painting of a wooden table over which few liquor bottles were kept and they were trying to know the brand name if they are familiar with or not. So after enjoying this preplanned drama leaving this shop owner and his paintings my eyes again concentrated on the streets.

The crowd in the streets was showing its huge presence in other hand the intense of the noon light was losing its strength. So many heads where halting and moving but in between them there was a color in major proportion, I noted. That was black yes black, acting as a black mark moving on the streets. Those were Muslim women's who were wearing black burkas, a long piece of clothing that covers the face and body, worn by them in public places in order to hide their physical beauty from the eyes of other males leaving husband and families as a ritual. The burka was covering them from tip to toes with a breach opening for their eyes in their niqab a part of burka covering their head. In this black attire from the breach opening of their face their beautiful alluring black almond eyes impressed my vision, I smiled. The fluttering big eyelashes, mascara lined up on their eyelids dashes, their piercing eyes, and their skin ton of pure milky white altogether gave an effect of an elusive, breath taking flower showcased forever. Wisdom of a lady her sleeves and curves her bent and bows not able to present how unfortunate I thought. Collectively if I see somewhere those eyes heavy-lidded eyes she is using as a sword, to give a seductive sparkle to make a man fell in love with them or What else they can do? What they have to show except a big black mark. Nothing! Then I considered if a word beauty is removed from the world of women kind, then what they can be called? A faded flower is about to fall.

There I was beginning to lose my temper in order to feel relaxed, I lighted a cigarette. There from the balcony again fumes took me with the flow of crowd and shown me another lady of same black burka hope. She was holding her small little boy of hardly five, halting, buying and negotiating from shop keepers aside. The lady was lean and thin with bewitching pie-eyes and the applied mascara gave her breathtaking ties. I released my fume smoky dunes, where rest else was totally covered in her burka looms. But somewhere I felt sympathy on her as she might be of 22 or 23 or even less. An age of blossom her beauty might be awesome but she was totally packed like a packet as she only belongs to some ones parcel. Like her so many black spots I had seen roaming here and there on the streets. It felt just like a flower is covered with a big black blanket who will wilt someway in some day but it will wilt soon is because of this blanket.

There in the balcony I imagined myself inside a blanket, feared. For hours days and years with a little opening somewhere in the blanket teared. Definitely I will feel suffocated bobbed and my trembling mind will throw it away to fire in coal never ever to be used for any religious roothold. The freedom I got, I will feel it to celebrate, by a quick warm up, I will try to feel I am free I am free I am free hhhfuu. But if I think about these women's they are made to wear these costumes for hours in a day and they have to continue this wearing as a ritual throughout their life. How they might be feeling pleasant, jacked might be captured.

The only word I can spell for this kind of brutal custom is illiteracy and inhumanity. What kind of community is this?

Where a woman is covered with a big black gown to hide from whom? From those male's who are behaving as a freedom bird, by suppressing those women's as they belongs to their ancestral property. Is this a faith or madness?

Where the preference for male is like he is born as sovereign where as value for female is as enervated pain. Then where is the term equality?

Where bloodshed is ritual to get heaven after death and freedom to walk speak see think enjoy is a mark of sin for a way towards hell. No one knows what after death, then why the people are fighting in this living life in the name of life after death, to make hell here onwards?

Where each part of life is restricted by imposing some rules, to follow as a tied up wound is the only way to know the purity in soul. But at last directly or indirectly the whole burden comes under women's as an axed wood.

Where women is considered as a machine, that gives high productivity with less maintenance cost if gone ill or become use less then get the new one are the only words.

Where instructions flow as hymns as rhymes from birth to death in perfect times. Where men are considered as king of humans and women's as slaves, in term a never ending tussle for most beautiful kinds. They are trying their best to believe it as a test, that they wish to pass by following those same hymns and rhymes a perfect and inviting way for more puzzles directly in their heavenly well, restricted and protected by the same attacker carrying bloody sword, a hanging bell.

Here everything depends on faith and belief for each day and nights even in sleep. In their rules there is no name and sign of humanity for relief. If it is not there then it should be renovated at least and if it is not possible, then we should throw out these feral rules from our dianain earth for the sake of human belief. People of this community first they should feel human inside them, then anything else for the enhancement of their religious kingdom. There is an exercise for these type people who are bounded with these kinds of belief and following like blinds. They can do it every morning and definitely it will work out, to feel humanity inside them. They can close their eyes where ever they are for some seconds or minutes. Now touch yourself, your hands, your thighs, your chest, stomach, face smoothly lovely and feel the smoothness of your flesh and the strength of your bones. You will feel, we are also a creature of this earth like ant's animal's birds and fishes. We are humans a creature from many of this earth but the difference is we have proper functioning brain use it in a correct way, for humanity not like animals harming each other with no sense of reality.

Things are changing day by day according to the trend due to modernization. But here in this community everything is same from last many centuries. The result is women of this community lost her ability to judge what is right and what is wrong. In a way she is confused whether she should wear this black burka or not. The twist is, yes she will wear and if any one comes to objects them. She will give a heart breaking answer "This is our right" on what basis they don't even know. And it is not their fault because if a look back we make in these women's life. It is black, a familiar color that they know from their childhood and still they know in the name of religion. But one day they will relies what mistake they are doing and continuing when they will feel a word captured from inside them.

There in the balcony by closing my eyes the last golden puff I hailed it took me inside where her darkness a hide. The sweat inside were rolling shied but the sun light in sky was smiling wide. My blinking eyes had seen the world, a freedom light in limited sight. Women's in sarees girls in geans how airy they feel I am suffocating plight. There beauty in crowd, people are appreciating loud. Is there any one to see my eyes, my beautiful eyes I applied mascara isn't it acknowledgeable sight, passed people never replied but my husband replied every night I am beautiful in sight for his use as a sexual right but no one seen my weeping eyes the pain inside laying wide inside a hide blasting cried.

Yes I remember those days our childhood days, we played hide and seek such a memorable days. Memories lighted my smiling face when others praised "A wining bay never ready to stay". Each time I hide a darkest place I took. Where no one can think, such a place I took. But I never imagined this darkness of my hide will overlap my life with a burka tomb, that I got when something broke inside me they called it as "Freedom Bond". From their onwards my captured body captured soul never uttered a single word against this burka or against this faith in fear of grave I know they are ready to make. But I uttered in a way I can say, in form of fragments we used as attar, hoping it can spell our pain strong and better in the crowd as attar (Perfume).

I released my fumes from the balcony height over the streets over the crowd as her fragment in air it's me desire, to whom should I pray? To whom should I obey? Who will give me a freedom day? These English streets of jeans and tees, I like to wear I swear but my covered body covered face never able to face any races. Today money is education but not made for us, because a place where crowded with siblings. We as a female always need to adjust, thinking that let them touch the tip of Himalaya we will wait, one day it will melt. They said home is home your dear home a responsible mom should not roam and from there onwards to go outside to have the sunrise is like, dream come home. Decoration and ornamentation is only known to our eyes as rest of the part is hidden toys, only known to play till sunrise. At first those were enjoying nights but very soon it felt a nail is hammered wild. We are two our two constitution says but our religion says we are two our ten and twenty years gone waste, as a loading truck we have to work until it stucks. We live in darkness from morning till night but that is not sufficient for men called giant, he imposes rules for each and every step we move.

My child hold my finger tight, crowd is there you will miss my sight and you will never be able to find me, because as like me many are there in this burka sight, a fight of women's in dark light. My child you are a boy, a freedom kite as well his need for futures fight. You as a "He" is always right. But this religious fight we will continue "she" as a dark light and we will be there inside this burka as captured world always in sight.

Dropping the fitter I opened my eyes. The mother and child went somewhere leaving a word captured world.

Hari Das

Captured World

Saudi Kings O Cruel Kings
Rules are rule made to rule
But over ruled

Burka war or Burka bar
What kind of tar

Captured eye
Will not see the sky?

Captured face
 Should not face a gaze?

Is it a value?
Is it a game?

Mr. we are humans
Touch the vein
You dirty drain

Are you a King?
Or a manqué being
We are women
Not an animal being

People in belief
Men are freaks'
Modernization in peek
But she is still so week

He held her hand
She thought a magic wand
A reflection for a stand
But where in this deserted land
Where he captured her
As a boutique in Finland

She will release her nature
She will release her pain
She will laugh here
Inside a burka
With a black name

Where

His dirty fire
Needs her as a black Safire
In an open fire
Yes

His dirty fire
Needs her white nude attire
In a room
As my lonely fire
Yes

His dirty fire
Needs her skin to glow

As he want to wow
Tough to go
A sexual Ohhh
This penile fight
Will never let her fly

This penile fight
Will never leave her alone

As she is also in a belief
With a penile treat
My family is my world
Where everyone is happy
In my safe hold
Even if I don't
Who cares for a Cole?

I will sleep anywhere
As I don't need the sunshine

As I don't need men as mine
My beauty is mine
For he as a dine

I will sleep anywhere
In any cornered room
Where he will room zoom
And boom

I am only a shining full moon
In a black deserted sky
Where my desires are eclipse
Without a star
Without a noon
In a captured world
In a captured world

Poetry is music a rhythm so read it lovely and smoothly

Hari Das

Need-3

It was 3'o clock in the evening and I was there in the balcony dreaming. Don't know how this mush of time went. This was my problem if I am there in the balcony I lose myself with the curse of the world. Day after tomorrow my first math paper was there but I dint even went to solve a single numerical up till that time. Because I know that somewhere inside me I was planed that I will not prepare for this math subject, as it was so difficult. Where from last two months I was trying to open this math subject but leaving it for a continues tomorrow there I was in a condition where only one day was left and this one day was not sufficient to pass this subject. So I leaved it for next semester as a back log thinking that I will see it there and the rest four subjects were theory there was no issue in studying that.

By the time I was starving for food and I was already late from the lunch timing. So quickly from the balcony I made a look in search of food if I could see any kind of restro in my street only. Fortunately I found two vegetarian restaurants aside to each other in front of my lodge which were near to the tea stall. I made a brief glance over these two restro's to select one of them. In the first restro an old man was sitting in his lobby waiting for the customer to arrive. From my balcony I could see two to three tables of his restro that were ready to be occupied but it was totally dark there in his restro as the light were switched off might be to reduce the electricity bill where as in the second restro adjacent to it a fat man was sitting in his lobby by giving his back to the old man in the first restro. Here the fat man was not idle he was calculating something in his diary might be about his daily collections where this restro was slight bigger than the first one. In comparison to tables I could see four to five and they were vacant as the peak time of lunch was over. The lights were on in this restro due to which it was clearly visible that how much neat and clean the floors and tables were. The salad plates, pickles and glasses were kept in the center of the table that showed everything is there in its correct place. By seeing his proficiency I hoped I can get good food here. So at the end I decided I am going to visit this restro it would be better rather than visiting that dull man's restro where everything was dark.

I locked my room had the staircase and I was there on the streets. After a little walk from the tea stall when I was just going to cross the street I read a board hooked up in the fat man's lobby facing towards me. It was written as a tag line of the restro

For 50 rupees limited food
For 60 rupees unlimited food

After reading this the word unlimited clicked in my head but I dint went for any second thought. In hurry I just crossed went inside had a seat facing towards the street and the fat man. Then I asked the fat man who was still busy in his calculations can I have a plate of 60 please. As soon as he heard he turned his head towards the kitchen and in loud voice he ordered his food supplier "a plate of 60 unlimited" get it fast. Then he again went into his calculations. My mouth began to water for the delicious food going to arrive. Where somewhere I was hoping with the word unlimited that the plate would be arriving will be full of rice spelling from the corners, many chapattis would be kept over the rice hanging in one side with its weight as it is just going to fall and three to four bowls filled with different kind of vegetable curies. So I started waiting curiously. During this time for an instance my eyes went on that fat man. It seemed he dint went for shave from last many days his white beard told and as a sign of aging little bit of wrinkles were there in his round face. Can be denoted as an Uncle who was there in his 50's, his hair was black might be using godrej hair color to look young but his skin tone was pure cream which indicated that he is from a high cream layer class family who only knows one thing to sit and earn. He was wearing neatly pressed yellow kurta and pagama with a thick golden chain in his neck hanging and so many golden rings in his fingers in both of his hands to show I am a rich fellow but physically he was a fat man with overweight more than 100 kg if I am shore or like a real Indian business man I can say.

There after two minutes finally the plate arrived but it was not according to my assumptions that I calculated. There were only three chapattis but thick and big with four bowls of vegetable curies and good sufficient amount of rice in one corner with curd sprinkled over it. For a second to clear my confusion I asked to the waiter guy what's the difference between 50 and 60 plate exactly. What he said is in 50 you will get 5 chapattis with rice and curies and in 60 you can eat unlimited chapattis. After hearing this I relaxed myself by uttering this word Unlimited in an excitement. Soon my watering mouth loosed its control and there I began to eat. One by one the chapattis finished then two more arrived I ate that also, by the time I was feeling that I am done as the chapattis were very heavy and thick. I thought if I am going for the sixth one, I would not be able to eat rice. So leaving chapatti I had the rice mixing dal and other curries left in the bowls with some salad and pickle mixed hmm it was tasty. So finally I was done with my food and I was feeling energetic. Very soon there I washed, paid and went off. Next day I again came here before my first paper at noon slight earlier at 12:30 for my lunch. Some people where already having their food. There I occupied a safe corner before the restro get filled. But this time I went for 50 Rs plate that means limited because I had a 50 rupees note with me, thinking that then no need to break down a 100 rupee note and I can save it.

In few minutes the plate arrived and there I was having my food. One by one again the chapattis began to finish but this time while having my fifth chapatti suddenly something clicked. In a confusing manner I felt something somewhere is wrong yes. If I see, I am having the same quantity of food that I had yesterday in 60 Rs plate consisting 5 chapattis with curies and rice. There I recognized one of my mistake which I did yesterday and that was I only had five chapattis in unlimited where I can go for the sixth one also but I dint. That means yesterday I had a plate of 50 Rs only and still 10 Rs were left that I wasted. But in 50 only I got this much of sufficient food with heavy big 5 chapattis with curies and rice that an above average man like me will never go for the 6th one, I am shore. That means that 10 rupees directly went to his pocket. And if I would see in a way, if a new costumer is arriving in this restro definitely he will go for 60 Rs plate by getting attracted from this tag line of "For 60 Rs unlimited food", that's what I did. And in a crowded street like this how many number of new costumer would be arriving unlimited.

I was stunned, when I found that, it was a cheap marketing trick this fat man is using to fool the peoples in the name of limited and unlimited to earn extra profit of 10 Rs per client. He knows that if a person is going for 60 Rs plate he can eat food of 50 Rs plate only so that the left 10 Rs can be his extra profit. It means if the real profit is 20 Rs then this trick is giving him extra 10 Rs so that it can be a major profit of 30 Rs per client. Finally I understood the tag line of this restro.

For 50 rupees limited food
For 60 rupees unlimited food

I felt myself as a donkey who went into his trap by himself at first time only. I should have gone for 50 Rs plate yesterday but I loosed my 10 Rupees it's not a big sum somewhere. But If I think about each customer arriving who might be going for 60 Rs plate. Then per day how much huge profit he might be earning. Then I got the thing why this fat man is always busy in his calculations without even going for his shave. At last after completing my food I paid him with a cruel eyes and a sorrow of losing 10 Rs made me to think how greedy and needy he is even though he is a rich fellow. Definitely he might be eating the left food of his restro by himself only that's why he became this much fat. Now what kind of other stunts he might be using in food quality too was a big question. I went out deciding will never come back here again. While moving towards a square near by the mobile market his face was rolling in my head like a thief who stoles money technically by fooling peoples.

There after reaching that square I took a seat in a tea shop while having my tea and fumes I went into a thought. How people can be this much busy to earn. Is this word money has this much of important in life? And if it is yes, then "Is that human is driving the money or money is driving the humans". To get an answer my eyes went into the streets. In the eyes of those street side shop owners and people around me in that square I had seen a term seek, a wait in their eyes. That they are doing for money to fulfill their needs. Their need that is never ending because it took a form of greediness which will be there in side them until there last breath. Yes I had seen they are in wait, in seek, in hurry, and running behind this word "money" who is their driver to achieve everything in life.

Crores and millions of people are there in this world and they are going to office and work every day. In that most of the people are doing same kind of work every day as like a repeat or copying each day like that fat man who indulge himself in his everyday calculations to earn profit. One day it will become there part of life and the easiest thing they can do in order to pass their time. And one day life will pass; they won't even know how it passed. When a look back they will make they will feel guilty that they were after money thinking that fulfillment of life is fulfillment of needs otherwise what you lived.

Life means need it will never rest it will keep on growing which in term will give you a struggle, hard work, and lots of tension to achieve the things that are only human made.

A need is an endless road in which our each foot step will spell a word money and if we are into it. Then our thinking will travel in a way "How to earn?" if earned then "Profit?" if earned the profit also then "more and more" and it will continue up till our end of life. As a result at the time of death sadness with lots of regret will capture us due to our unfulfilled needs and at last we will die as hopeless.

> **"A *Need is a Restless Seed***
> ***Whether it is Small or Big***
> ***It is Need"***
>
> *Hari Das*

Life can be too easy if we think. For this we have to understand our existence in life in term "A start has an end" that means we are born to die. But with this pace of life people get forget that they are in the direction of death as this need took place as a seed. One day this seed will immerge out as a plant, then as a tree and it will keep on growing with so many branches, flowers and fruits then as a nest for birds. In reality this tree in form of need is acting as a wall in between their life and death.

The person who is busy in fulfilling his never ending needs can't see his death coming closer to him is because this wall of need is hiding his death. And when it comes fear began to grab his legs because he doesn't know the meaning of word acceptance in term "He is not ready to accept his death or He doesn't want to die because his needs are still left to be fulfilled". Now to overcome this fear he will choose a path which gets him into the direction of belief. That tells, you will get heaven after death if you will follow our rules but what you did for people and humanity to get heaven also. You were busy in fulfilling your needs.

The word acceptance is a stability to balance our needs. It means the clothes we wear can be cheap or expensive but what is the purpose to hide our nudity. The food we eat can be cheap or expensive but what is the purpose to anguish our hunger. The place we live can be a bungalow or a small house but what is the purpose to isolate yourself and family to maintain privacy from rest of the world. This is called a peace full life or a streamlined flow of life like a straight line from start to an end by carrying fewer needs. Here an end of a person who had less needs, will be awaited by himself hopefully with pleasure to rest in peace because all his needs are fulfilled that were acting as a wall for him, that he already removed in his gone back days and submitted himself to this nature and earth thankfully.

If you see around us there is no one to give us a single penny when we are in need. Earn that much that you can accept "not even more not even less" to fulfill our sufficient needs. If you have more donate it for those who are in need without any hope of return.

Those rich people in the society and community for whom each day is a new day, in a way of most expensive dresses, cars, food in five star hotels and a lavish expensive tours and travels. If they will think for a second just ones and avoid buying a new dress worth of lakes only one time, that money can root up a child from street to a class room where the child can get a good education for his bright future and all other basic elements for a standstill in between the society and community.

Those homeless people who are lying in the foot paths recklessly as an avoided fellows from the society, communities and from that government who is busy in developing a country of baseless structure. Who is going to accept them shamefully nobody is there.

Some where these people are annoyed with the ill-fated life they got with no support and help from any one of them they are living on the streets. Now if we see this homeless people living in streets in a different way, by avoiding these sentimental emotions of week and poor. They are in strike on the foot paths, busts tops, and many other places with long beards untidy cloths and with an ugly face they are waiting for a call from someone some day they are hoping it will arrive. Yes it will arrive they are thinking and waiting. And when it will arrive their eyes will glitter with new tears of hope to live and be happy again in life. It is same as those children playing in a garden in which a child is made out from a team is because he was not performing well and where he is sitting in a nook of the garden in a fit of anger with sorrow in his heart hoping that someone will call him back. Please

Call them just "ones"
Spend it just "ones"
Save a life "ones"
And give a perfect end to a life "ones"

So many are there in various parts of the streets who are waiting just for an helping hand. They are also our needs as a contribution to the society and state for a better future and life.

"If You Know the Seventh Heaven of Having
You should also Know the Pleasure of Giving"

Hari Das

I know, one day the fat man in his old age will regret because he doesn't know his existence in his life, his limit for his earning. He doesn't know the meaning of word acceptance because he is running behind his needs. One day he will know when his death will arrive he can't take away any of the things what he earned and achieved from his need and greediness of his life. He will know he is only going to submit his soul and body to the almighty of darkness and nature. But unfortunately he will feel he is too late and he will regret for losing his precious time of happiness and easiness that he spent for his needs.

Hari Das

Nandini

My name is Nandini
I sell pens in the traffic signal
When the signal get orange'd
I sell pens long and elastic pens

I move door after door
Carrying bunches of pen

I knock on the door
Five a pen for ten three pens
But no one buys
They tell we have a pen
Small and fountain pen

I don't know how to write
How to read
But i know how to sell these pens

Someone buy someone buy
Five a pen for ten three pens

Child in door shining pen
Mamma i need i need this pen
Long and elastic pen

How much for a pen?
My age is five
Five a pen for ten three pens

One i sold
Still left in fold

Someone buy someone buy
Five a pen for ten three pens

Bunches of pen i carry
With each dip of the sun
When the foot paths belong to rich
In between the short skirts white lady's
In between the family's holding small baby's
I carry pens bunches of pen
Long and elastic pens

Sometimes
Waving hands discard me
Go away with your pen long and elastic pen
We don't need your pen
Your dirty pen
Pen

But i have to raise my hands
From the evening till dark
Because the morning is not going to gift me
A school to use this pen
So i only know to sell these pens

Someone buy some one buy
Five a pen for ten three pens

My name is Nandini
I sell pens in the traffic signal
When the signal get orange'd
I sell pens long and elastic pens

Poetry is music a rhythm so read it lovely and smoothly
Hari Das

<u>If</u>

If there is a forest
There is a barren land

If there is darkness
There is a sourcing light

If there is belief
There is a term relief

If there is disbelief
There is a term self

If there is good
There is a bad

If there is human
There is air to breath
Water to drink
Food to eat

Everything is there in this nature
With an if
With an else

But if there is a start
There is an end.....

Poetry is music a rhythm so read it lovely and smoothly

Hari Das

Belief-4

Days began to pass and the exams were going good leaving math but still two papers were left. After leaving that shop I found a new spot for my food. It was a Chinese stall a hawker who was providing Chinese food in very cheap rate with good quantity in plate as well it was very tasty and spicy too. I continued to have food from here for noon and evening time. Sometimes I eat fried rice or Manchurians or noodles that were only costing 30 Rs per plate. The stall was near to my lodge in a square before the mobile market and after imily gali. In this square it was installed on the edges of a wide divider, in one of the street of this square in which at the dead end, a mosque was there where as in the opposite street of this mosque street a temple was there at the square only.

It can be said as Temple square so in this temple square at evening time because of availability of various types of market in its connecting streets huge rush of public would be there slight more from the afternoon time with heavy flow of traffic. The pedestrians and the customers like me who are staying in lodges prefer to come here to have this delicious Chinese food prepared in front of us by two Assami guys.

Day before my fourth paper in the afternoon time the intense of the sunlight was very high where on that day India had won the cricket match from Pakistan that left a twinkling smile over the faces of public with a cheerful atmosphere and a brief talk about the cricket match was going on everywhere on the streets. In this afternoon time I was having my fried rice sitting in a small stool of this Chinese stall at the edges of Mosque Street opposite to Temple lane. There after sometime when I was in the mid portion of my lunch I heard some drum beats with ry-thmetic style of bangara was playing somewhere on the streets of this square. The drum beats began to come closer and closer that everyone in the square gets attracted towards the beets. On hearing closure it was exactly coming from the opposite street of temple line. Soon a group of youngsters emerge out from the temple street with three to four drummers carrying Indian national flag to celebrate the victory made by Indian team against Pakistan. The drummers increased their pace of beating through that a riotous sound entered in the atmosphere that changed the state of square from a numb state to pleasant and heart full state. The youngsters began to dance with the beats by waving the flag in one side and raising slogans of high spirit in another side. There after shop owners of street side by closing their shops and public from various parts of the streets began to join this thesaurus atmosphere as a result in few minutes the small group turned into a huge crowd. In this crowd now some people were throwing flowers over the people who were dancing but somewhere I noted their eyes of each one of them at a certain point of glance were clashing with the eyes of public standing by my side who were of different community. From my side also people began to gather of other community and were watching these people who were laughing and dancing but with a gloomy face and fierce eyes without a single smile in any one of the face. There I felt somewhere a dispirited atmosphere was there among them in my side. An old lady by my side near to me was talking to her son continuously without giving a single glance over the celebrating public who where there in front of her only. At this point somewhere in her eyes I found a sense of fear which she was trying to hide.

People were gathering in both the side continuously that if I see in my side men where in pathanis(a type of traditional dress of Muslims) and in another side men's in shirt pants and kurta pajamas(a type of traditional dress Hindus). Soon I felt I am there in between a vibrant and a dull troupe. If I guess strongly, soon the situation changed into a state of showoff where both the troupes were trying to show their strength to words each other. And there I understood a source of tension is hidden somewhere in this atmosphere and it can explode at any time. A sense of panic began to grip my feet and there suddenly my mind insisted me to move away from this jeopardy atmosphere. So I finished my food very quickly and after paying I leaved the spot because I know at any time the situation can go under control in form of communal violence that usually happens in this country during these types of matches of India and Pakistan.

By leaving the spot I entered in my street of lodge's imily gali. In between the people in the crowd I loosed myself with the flow of other footsteps. Different faces with different races passed by me that manipulated my eyes and went into their attire another differentiating sight. In their wearing I sensed a belief that they were following as a hope of relief. Their clothes spelled he is there who gifted me life to believe him is my natural right because he will save me in each part of the life. Belief took the people in a depth of a sea now it is impossible to rope back from this trippy sea. They will live there by thinking I am right because we left the wrong which was a freedom light. People are fighting to claim their belief, that our belief is right and rest else is wrong but who knows, who is right and who is wrong.

People only made this right and wrong which travelled the whole earth in different zones, where humans took the right by neglecting the wrong as a mark of sin which was always thorn and amended this right with different names which in term called religion a correct way of life clamed.

The tension I got in the name of belief now I could see everywhere in the market street. In the bindi stuck over forehead of a woman, over the cap and burka of Muslim men and women's, on the saffron dress of a pundit in common, on a cross hanging in a chain of a men uncommon, from everywhere different kind of belief began to clash in my eyes. I went into my room with my fumes inside, I went into a thought for clarification I need.

To know this terminology of belief I asked to myself. What is the existence of belief in our life tell me my soul, tell me what it says my guru. I closed my eyes for a answer I need the darkness of my eyes took me to into space from where I had seen the bluish earth where our world resides.

From here if you see the world we all people are there in a circuit connected to each other. It's like a circuit of many junctions connected to each other via tiny nerves or bridges and the base of this circuit is the world and nature.

Each junction of this circuit is a person who is connected to other junctions via nerves or can be called bridges that in term can be called as relations like family friends acquaintance or sometime stranger can also get connected. These nerves took suggestions given by one junction to another junction or person, that in term will act as a path of life that where he should move next in the circuit by leaving this junction to another junction so that he/she can meet more person or junction to give and take suggestions to get an end of life.

These suggestions are instincts or a message given in between soul and a person then from one person to another person that will act as next step of his/her life in order to move in the circuit towards an end of life.

Now to know these instincts or a message, first you have to believe you're self it means believe your soul as like you believe in God, and then know your inner peace and silence of your soul or mind which is a positive energy inside you and it knows everything about you who you are? For what you are? What you can do? What you have to do?

This inner peace and silence of your soul is an energy that has a power to see the coming future of yours and others too in form of instincts as a message delivered by our soul to us. If you know this energy inside us, you will smoothly flow in the circuit. These instincts can connect you to the world and nature and can plot a graph for your life with others.

To know this energy which is inside you as a soul you don't have to go anywhere in any Temple Church or Mosque. Just close your eyes for a while and feel the silence and peace inside you and ask yourself who I am? Or If any problem" This is my problem please help me my soul please help me". And the acknowledgment you will get automatically in a way that your soul will connect you from this world and nature and through various happenings your soul will deliver you an instinct or a message which is an answer by your soul to you or your wishes that you demanded to your soul that automatically get fulfilled because your soul will connect to this world and nature and make the situations in favorable for you and if it is not possible to come in favor then also it will deliver a message for you in form of Yes or No in your darkness of your eyes.

Now if you know yourself that means you can feel your soul, it means now you can know others too because you know the energy inside you it can connect with the energy of another person that will give you an instinct a message in form of images in your eyes or in form of words or any other sign or happenings. And there you read the next person without sharing a single word with him, now you can acknowledge him as a suggestion an instinct to give him a direction towards his end of life but the most important thing is you should know your inner peace and silence very well such that your suggestions or instinct should never went wrong.

Ex:- if you see these animals why they know that the natural calamity is going to arrive is because they know there soul better with a perfection that they can connect with the nature and get the messages as an instinct and then try to show us in their own way as a sign that never went wrong.

All these things people know but not in correct form because our ancient people what they did is they termed those people who know this energy inside them as God, Alla, Bhagvan and with many others names because what they acknowledge it was future it was past it was humanity it was for good and a way towards end of life.

But for normal people it was unbelievable because they were not capable to understand or dint tried to know the energy inside them. So they became followers. Then in the coming days and years they termed those godly man as a religion a belief, cast, custom, creed and now in the name of them temple, churches, mosques ,ashrams are made and now they are also called as saints of god.

**"I have a question for these peoples
They always say "He is there"
"He is there"**

But why not "She is there"

"She is there"
Tell me?"

I will tell you:-

He is there inside us in form of grandfather father brother son friend husband etc

She is there inside us in form of grandmother mother daughter sister friend wife etc

These all relations are bridges or the thin nerves towards one junction to another junctions or person as a relation in the circuit.

I had seen my father who usually prays in front of a small temple in our home. At that time I see him carefully when he mutters in front of the temple by joining his hands. Where at that time my mind trembles to say him you are talking to yourself there is nothing in front of you else than a rock. Exactly what you are thinking that the energy of divines is there inside that rock or photos or somewhere in the atmosphere but it is there inside you only.

If you ask to your soul, tell your problem to your inner peace it will never be unanswered because your soul is your driver in this circuit of life. But what the people did is they transformed their energy to a rock or moon or wood that can't answer anything and there the life will pass away in waiting for the answers with so many confutations in life.

Try to know your inner peace and silence it has all the answers what you need. As like you pray to the god, pray to your soul in the darkness of your eyes "what is your problem tell to your Soul and there you see the effect of your soul definitely it will work out. I am shore. One day people will know this energy inside them and then there will be only one belief Our Soul. "After knowing this energy inside them I believe one day people will become that much efficient that they can understand what their soul speaks "It speaks what's going to come and happen". If they can listen or understand their soul then they can also give suggestions to others and will be able to take right suggestions from others who know this energy of peace and silence inside them in order to get an end of life.

The person who understand life definitely he will understand the energy inside us.

Hari Das

Belief

My feet in Streets
Walking Latif
Races and Faces
Clashes Lashes

Hashish in Reef
There the passing Feet's
Difference in Attire
Fumes said Belief
Belief Belief

Human Arrived
Clothes Derived
Clothes Named
Difference Aimed
Human Changed
Brain Drained
Religion Came

Religion a Host
Host a Cost
For humanity in Clothes
My eyes Wows
Ghost

Poetry is music a rhythm so read it lovely and smoothly

Hari Das

Maulana

A Maulana in town
White shirt
Long Beard
Was his gown

Morning color
With praying flower
Allah in Heaven
His perfume
Was Amen

Walking on the streets
His stick of teak
Color of week
Sounded peek

White cap rounded other caps
With a shimmer in smile
Allah hafiz
He mild

His fragment in town
In orange gown
A pundit (Sag) was passing
Nearby his gown

He interrupted with hello
Smile ello
But his head drowned
No reply he found

O my mistake, My Lord
He prayed in haven
Perhaps
Who cares in Town

Pundit (Sag) in his way
Flowers for the day
Freshness smells
Fragment of rose
Purity is most
At any cost

Maulana in his way
Spells for the day
He is there in smile
He is there in words
I love my lord
In pure words

Poetry is music a rhythm so read it lovely and smoothly

Hari Das

A Deflection

Hunger-5

My thoughts traveled way back from the world of belief where a clarification I made and satisfied myself. Then I again went into my studies for my fourth paper from where I left before the lunch. Next day it was 6'o clock in the evening just came into my room after giving my exam. My long continues hard work of last day worked and my paper went good. Now a last paper and two more stays in Bhopal was left but a little bit mawkish I felt because the street atmosphere I got here it was tempting and mind blowing. The days went made me connected with the streets and people residing here now to leave this place was the toughest job I felt I have to do. Any way after an hour between 7 and 7:30 as my routine I was planned to move for my usual walk and at the end a dinner at that Chinese stall. So before that I took a nap because I was totally tired from the long travel I made in a tightly stuffed auto rickshaw from my college till this lodge.

Somehow one hour passed and I woke up with my struggling hands then any how I readied myself and I was there on the streets again. Illuminated bulbs of street lights and shops exhibited that market is still busy in selling their products but soon the market will close down for the next coming day. Crossing the street I reached at my usual spot at temple square for dinner in that Chinese stall and took a seat by ordering fried rice. As I was noticing from last many days that these Assami guys are earning huge from this Chinese stall. The coming and going passers in a curiosity took pause at this stall to taste this Chinese food and later on they become their regular customers as I had become. It was because these guys are from north eastern state of India and the people from this state are really good in cooking especially Chinese food. It arrived in India from our neighboring country china and these north eastern state people who live nearby border of china took it as their business of Chinese foods and now it is widely spread all over India in form of these kind of stalls by these peoples that is now common and cheaply available in various part of the streets.

The fried rice that I am going to have can be called indo Chinese food. In this the major ingredient is rice specially basmati rice half cooked in which finely chopped veggies are added like carrot beans spring onions button mushrooms spice star anise capsicum garlic cabbage leaves few boiled soya bean balls or pastas and the most important ingredient of Chinese food cereals otherwise it will feel something is missing then over it spices are added to give a spicy taste like red chilly green chilly with salt and pepper. Now all these things are souted in a pan with little bit of cooking oil to give smoothness. When the brownish color arrives in rice and veggies then soya souse is added for a flavor. So finally it means little bit of more soute and there it is ready to be shifted in a plate. The taste is hot and spicy with robustness of all veggies maintained.

At last my wait finished and the stemming vegetarian fried rice plate arrived, over it I squeezed tomato souse then I took my first spoon and it was always un chewable for me is because of my hurry to taste I forget that it is hot. I waited for few seconds to cool down then started eating spoon by spoon frantically that at a sudden point of glance in front of me I loosed my pace of eating and chewing when a whimper I heard from a small desolated homeless boy standing in front of me. I saw his tongue twisting over his lips with a watery mouth to know the taste of my rice. Where his dull faded eyes with a big tied up wound in his forehead was strictly pointing towards my food and in a mercy he was begging in front of me with his fingers wide opened stretched towards me. Now it was not possible for me to eat in front of a starving child in a way it was totally an awkward situation. I felt agonized from the facial expression I got from the child and his big tied up wound in his forehead frightened me I thought who might be that person who had beaten a child in such a cruel manner definitely he might be a coldblooded savage or it can be he might had met with some kind of accident whatever but this wound seems terrible. By seeing his horrible condition there my mind unexpectedly scripted some words and went into my past in my childhood.

> **"My eyes in sunder**
> **Hunger in finger**
> **His face as shunder**
> **How pity I wonder"**

Vision of that day came into my eyes when my family went for an evening out at city center in our city side. Clusters of people were arranged in streets passing by them in a jolly mood we were visiting stall by stall by having the street foods where I felt the taste is still there in my mouth. There in a particular stall we took a pause and ordered kachories (an Indian street junk food). Mom dad and we both twin brothers began to wait for the kachories to arrive. Then one by one as soon as it came. My father and brother took an immediate bite where as mom and I were not ready, we were just going to eat that few street children came in front of us by begging for food to eat. By seeing their exaggerated merciful pleading a sense of kindness evoked in mother's heart reluctantly she with affection passed her plate to a small girl who was youngest among them. And I too did the same act what mother did without thinking for what I am doing. But when mom eyed dad and brother with a hope that they should also offer them perhaps both of them moved back in a way that they are not ready to give. Somewhere my father dint liked the act what we did so he yelled on my mother can't you see people are there around us they will offer them we don't have to do this it's not our duty. There my mother carried a stiff face and reacted in the same manner as father did. She said we are also a part of this crowd if others can forget their duty we can make them remember and it's not about our duty it's about our culture of giving and helping the unfortunates. Hearing this my father became impatient and in aggressive way he said to follow your culture I don't have that much of bank balance better you opt for some other way to help them but not with my money do you understand. She took mum state and dint went to react. There after a strong disagreement my father again ordered two more plates when it arrived unfortunately with that few other street children also arrived. Again by seeing their poor condition kindness of my mother count resist her, this time also she again offered her plate by un hearing the harsh words fired by my father being mother's pet I too did what she did but my brother was still eating his kachories fondly without bothering what's going on he was always there in fathers side. At last my father in a fit of anger said you both don't deserve this place common let's move now, next time please don't come to me in the name of outing I will not take you both anywhere hearing this brother smiled and chuckled.

From there the kindness of my mother came into me to react and I ordered another plate of fried rice for him. By tapping his back I said don't cry child you need food you will get ok but don't cry. In return he nodded his head a little with a blank expression in his face. He took the plate offered and by taking a safe corner he was eating where as I completed my food before him. I paid and went off with a relaxation of giving what my mother always does. The next day I came back at the same time where it was my second last day in

Bhopal. During the time when I was having my food this time three to four street children arrived in front of me. Acting as straight forward all of them stretched their hands towards me. At first I went into confusion what is this? Is that the yesterday's wounded child told his friends too that a kind man will arrive at this time and a merciful beg can get a hot and spicy plate of fried rice to eat very easily. To clear my doubt I moved my head in all direction to know whether the yesterday's boy is standing somewhere in hiding and might be peeping here to know what's happening there and checking the possibilities that at last he can also get a plate or not but fortunately no where he was. Then I thought if I am going to offer each one of them a plate it will cost a bit high and as well I don't have that much of sum with me just know. So I graphed my hands in my pocket how much coins I have I fetched it out and distributed to them where as soon as they got their offering they leaved the spot with no expression of even a thanks that I expected they will try to show.

After they went I continued my food while eating various thoughts began to tickle my head that provoked me to peep into my past life from my childhood till now. If I notice where ever I went from my childhood till now I found these kind of many street children roaming around somewhere on the streets. Their faded teared clothes filled with dirt always felt greenish in color. Their long hairs filled with dust and mud of streets which never under went for a scissor always felt greenish in color. Their stinky ugly face in which stains of last night food around their lips revealed how wild they were while eating last night food but never went for a wash to feel the taste in the next coming hunger by leaving a mark green in color. Blemishing mark of mire and cow dung on their dangling paws always look green in color. As this green is acting as a protective shield for these street urchins as a gift of world to be called as descendants of nature.

But is this shield sufficient for them for their whole life or to remove a difference between a normal child and a street grown up child. What after their childhood when they will lose their innocence in their teen age and adult hood when no one will offer them anything. Definitely they have to work and they will work hard but as a sweeper in trains, as a cleaner in street side cheap hotels, as a servant for rich, as helpers for street venders and the earning that they will get from their hard work

What they will do?
They will buy clothes? Or
Go for a hair cut? Or
Buy good food to eat?

As per I know what I had seen they will use them for their addictions for cheap drugs which they learnt from their childhood in order to overcome the feeling of starvations they will smell it hard to feel high and touch the glory of everything that they don't have and never going to get. If dint got any job they will join as goons for political king pines who are always waiting for such kind of fellows to hire. And what about the girl child what can happen with them after their puberty? As no one is going to offer them a job because what they need is pleasure they will get it by raping her again and again and then after use by showing the stars of love marriage and home they will sell them in brothels to end up as sluts or prostitutes. At last all of them will end up in jails as criminals.

But
Who made them beggars?
Who made them druggist?
Who made them prostitutes?
Who made them criminals?

We people our constitution our society our community who dint accepted them only donated them in form of coins and foods as offerings in fit of emotions to help them just to pass there life which I too did before some time. But all this type of donation is not going to help them because these are temporary satisfactions for a particular time being after that they have to be on the streets again to beg. But unfortunately no buddy is there to help them to get them a normal life like a normal child with love affection support regular food clothes home school & education college job marriage family a settled life but here all these things are absent in their life and what they only have is tears starvation begging and drudgery always waiting for them on the streets.

For them who is there?
Who is there?
NGO's

Is it but I don't think so because the way they are working it indicates they are not working for any cause other than money.

NGO's who are acting as a savvier for those diseased and affected people by various in humanitarian or natural and unnatural acts happened in their life with a big tag line non profitable non business and legally formed organizations.

The sponsors of these NGO's only know one thing is to donate donate and donate. Some people are donating heartily where as some people for a show in order to save tax or to call themselves as socialite in between the society and community. But all these kind hearted donors' never went for a thought to check whether their donated amount is reaching up to the diseased or affected in a correct manner or not because they don't care for anyone other than themselves. What they need is to call themselves as socialite that they got automatically as soon as they signed their checks and offered them. Another quality they got to add in their list of fake wisdom.

These donors' acts as innocent but literally they know that the funds that they are providing for a cause will be misused for which they don't care too. In a way when these funds are ready to flow for its final destination. For example: - Fund for an orphanage to buy one year grocery.

The fund donated will travel through various levels or channels from high to low level authority of that NGO. When it does the exact amount keep on decreasing after passing each level. And at last when it reaches in its final destination to execute the final goal or objective insufficient fund is left because each level ransacked the money thinking that who is going to ask for this donated amount. It is same as a piece of flesh is thrown by someone for a cat but unfortunately ten other dogs entered forcefully and ate that piece of flesh leaving a little bit as waste for the cat that is not at all sufficient to anguish his hunger.

So we can imagine that the grocery bought from that insufficient amount would be insufficient and can be of substandard quality or out dated. Due to such kind of deeds of authorities those orphanage children has to suffer by starving or by malnutrition. Here the whole act of NGO to fulfill the main objective was worthless or just a show "That it is done" but who is responsible for this? No one that is called NGO

Non Governmental Organization = No one is there to ask.
Non Profitable = Profit for the authorities working behind and loss for the children in front.
Non Business = Doing business by showing these ill fated people by both donors and NGO's.
Legally Formed Organization = Legal authority to stole money.

If we see as soon as a person steps into an NGO or even their website the first thing they will deliberately force us to do is donate. If we donated too does your each penny is used for the welfare of an individual what is the proof?

There is an another scenario if we see the cancer centers run by various NGO's who are getting huge support in way of money from the rich society. From that amount they are spending 5 to 10 or 15 lakh or more per patient in order to save a patient from cancer if it is curable because it is medically proven that up to 60% to 70% cancer cases are curable. Then also at the end after spending this much of fund with a major percentage of chance lying they are dying why? And if a person from rich society is suffering from cancer or any other chronic diseases they are not trusting Indian hospitals due to lack of medical facilities. They will visit America or any other developed country and spend 1 to 2 crore rupees or even more and get cured due to highly advance medical facilities available in that country and get saved.

But why dint they preferred India a big question? If they can't prefer India how a common man can trust the Indian hospitals. It means for them cancer means death arrived. The things going around in these centers is just a show an adjustment other than nothing because the hospital authority knows the funds arriving for the patient is insufficient and due to lack of medical facilities the only thing that they can do is show off. The patient dealing with these NGO's definitely they have to die they will die because they are not born in a golden cradle to stand out and deal by them self.

In this 20th era around 65% of NGO's are corrupted in India specially the branded NGO's. Whatever you donate only a least percent is reached up to the affected person. This was two of the scenarios of an NGO there are many in number if we analyze. Now we can imagine from this scenarios what could be the condition of Governmental Organization of India the real Indian government it could be worse than this.

Example: - The tsunami victims of 2004 for whom organizations like UN and our Indian Government allotted millions of dollars for the affected people of around 10 to 11 thousand but do you think the exact amount that should reach up to the victim has reached. If we give a close look it is in between reached and un reached because the victim only got 50000 to 1 lakh Rupees per person and for many even this amount also they dint got why? If the tsunami relief authority had distributed the exact amount each person should get at least 10 to 15 lakh or more with a concrete house to live but what they got exactly a bit of amount that is not even sufficient for a family for even 2 months with a tin sheet hut. Is this a relief or a fix done just to show the world? How devastating and shameful situation is this for this we should feel pity towards our old structured governance. But here the main question is where the money went? That everyone knows where it went but nobody is there to ask and defend. Who is there to blame those Tsunami relief authorities? No one is there same scenario as NGO's.

From all these things the major question arises is if the donated amount is not reaching up to the cause why we should donate? Should every one stop donating? Preferably No every citizen should if they have that much of capital to donate because we are responsible to help our human kind for their welfare. Now the person will thing why we are responsible because animals have limitations to give us in return the best answer he should know. If a person donated some amount there his responsibility doesn't ends there if he really cares that a cause has to be neutralized any how then he should check whether the exact Check In amount is Check outed or not. So that the sufferer can get the full benefit of this life saving amount in all manner. For this various IT companies should come forward and should provide an error free system or an independent NGO platform like portals with check in and checkout function with a bill generator. There the bill can act as satisfaction and a proof that for which person or child it was spent, what the utilities were bought etc.

Now if we look into the matter of these street children roaming here and there on the streets begging aside. There are so many NGO's in our country who are providing support for these street children but only if someone calls and inform them about a child. Then only they will come and pick up the child and think for his rehabilitation. Even though if an NGO is having space for a street child like out of 100 25 vacant space is there then also they will not try to fill this place else they will wait for a call to arrive when it will come automatically the space get filled is there thought. Now here is a question. Is this a correct way that an NGO should follow? Why they are waiting for a call? Why the volunteers of an NGO don't come by them self and hunt out these street children from the streets? Is this not there responsibility? If these question can be answered in a correct way there will be no street child left anywhere on the streets. Definitely they get saved. If there is no space in their NGO then they can contact another NGO for a support. Why NGO's for child welfare don't think in this manner? It means there first importance is donation for which they are sending their volunteers everywhere in the society to collect funds but not to hunt out a child. If got any one also they will act as unseen because no call is obtained. This is the basic reason due to which children with no support from anywhere surviving on streets.

Here the solution is simple if a city is having 50 NGO's for child welfare. Then if each NGO is deciding its area limit and picking up child from that area until no one is left then it means the area is free from street children. In this way if each NGO is working in this manner one day the whole city will be free from street child. For all these assumptions proper planning is needed but no one is going to do and follow as everyone need is money not these street urchins for them who care.

Suddenly I felt some one's hand tapping over my shoulders there I stood up leaving my chair in a shock and I found one of the Assami guy in front of me asking what happen to you sir is there any problem with my food. I was literally traumatized when I found myself sitting there in Chinese stall from an hour. The stall keeper noticed me wondering because I was not eating as well my eyes were staring somewhere concurrently in a numb state. I went into my though in such a deep state that I forgot that I am sitting there in a Chinese stall. In a sudden state I said ow I am sorry actually I just went into my thought but your food is excellent keep it up. In gratitude by complementing his food he said what can I do sir my food is like that people loss them self in the taste I provide any way have your seat and take your own time there is no problem. By giving thanks in a temperamental state I ate my food as soon as possible as I felt that I wasted my valuable time by thinking impossible things. At present I should be there with my chapters but I am there with this plate that is not fine. In hurry I completed my food paid and went off.

Next day last few hours were left in Bhopal in the evening time in an excitement I was sitting there in a bar with my four peg of Old Monk Rum waiting for me in my table. As I was eagerly waiting for this movement to get feel relaxed. So soon as I stepped out from my exam hall I was feeling exhausted though I was spending many days and nights in studies and streets indefatigable manner so I thought a feel good factor is needed. I went to my room packed my bags vacated the lodge by hiring an auto I reached here. In this dark atmosphere of bar first I felt sorry towards my father for not being there up to his point. Now what can I do such a wandering soul I have who likes freedom and to explain it to father, not my cup of tea. There I had my first peg. The effect I got began to fish out the past went days of Bhopal as a flash back. The mountains filled with greeneries bounding the cool water lake a magnificent site I had seen which took me into my past to My Lady with a galvanizing desire to see her ones for a last time but somewhere still left in my wish list as unfulfilled, releasing my fumes I said I will wait for you my My Lady like this fumes flying to trace an end. The second peg I had with this darkness of bar it remembered me the fight of women inside the burkas as applied tar. Hope the coming next century will vanish out these kind of brutality against women as a flood passed away from a village for a new lessons as upbringing waiting for them to arrive. I tipped my waiter before my third peg then I noticed my surrounding atmosphere. People were sharing their sorrows and pains with their companions aroused me to think. People and their needs is never going to end or balance but I know that my need is sufficient as pudina seed that has less growth but can give treatment if anyone in need and there I had my third peg. There after I raised my fourth peg in the name of belief that one day people will know themselves, that there will power is the most power full god present in side them, then they will not call any name of god other than inner soul that can answer everything in all. My last peg was also over but my soul insisted one more a last peg for my street urchins. Barer barer I chuckled and ordered one more last peg. There with my last peg in sorrow for those street urchins roaming here and there on the streets I began to sing my poetry in between that alcoholic atmosphere as On The Streets.

Hari Das

On-The-Streets

Born in black
I squeezed for the white milk
From an unknown Breast
On the streets
I was a month old as a feast (0-1)

I balanced my feat
Raised my hands for a treat
But nobody was there
To give me a warm great
She left me alone
With my future on the streets
But three year old that was least (1-3)

Streets took me to seek
To play hide and seek
I found some nomads
To roll down the tire on the streets
In the circus was the food as a fees
And for the people age six was sweet (3-6)

Cool breeze chilled our finger
White fog took shelter in the winter
Some where our teared cloths trendy in summer
Become first door to enter
We shivered on the streets
To stick to each other was least
Any how we have to pass the time
Because morning is going to gift us a warm shine

But we will find a place
Were we will beg for a sake
Can get some coins with woolen
From the rich people who pray's in heaven
And I will sleep with the age of nine
On the streets as lion (6-9)

Run run common fast on the streets
Said an ugly face to mugly face
Huge traffic is there to knock the door
Were I raised the voice as headline as a choice
If u need to know come and grab the voice

Mesmerizing to the god in each festive size
Something should happen somewhere
As I need to sell info with gear
So that at least today we can fulfill our hunger
As this age of eleven is not a big wonder (9-11)

Someone on the streets
Said we need to be protected
For the future of east
They took us to orphanage
Where everything was fine
With a show peace and a show time

Someone on the streets
Said we need to be protected more
For the future of east
So they took us to home
Were emotion was the trade mark
How much work we have to do
In the absence of the lady
Was a big question mark?

They took us as a dirty blood
As the real blood went to school
And we were left in the kitchens
Where broom act as a hunter
In each summer and winter

Blood shreds from the sky
Where each corner tells me to cry
For god sake I need my streets again
To hug my mother for a rain
As this age of fourteen
Is giving me unbearable pain
I need my streets again
I need my streets again
On the streets again......haaaa (11-14)

Poetry is music a rhythm so read it lovely and smoothly

Hari Das

Acknowledgment

I would like to thank following people for their valuable support throughout this journey of my life and book.

My Family

Father: Santhosh Kumar Mother: Shanta Kumari

Brother: Shreeju Panicker

Sisters: Karthika, Pooja

My Friend who is always dear to me

Ssabr Ulha Khan(srk)(Singer)

Freedom

Freedom my soul
I hold a gold
What i am i am
I am sold to my soul

Not like any one
I like to be one
Who knows his wisdom
Who knows his kingdom
There he is one
I am only one

A fire in gold
I love my soul
I am desire
My soul entire
My own sapphire
Polished attire

I know who i am
A human kind
Freedom bind
Born to leave
As refined

Poetry is music a rhythm so read it lovely and smoothly

Hari Das

NOTE

I am writing, not for today not for tomorrow, I am writing for the coming next 30th century. Here from streets I am trying to point out those negativities of this century that sometimes gives us sleepless nights. I am trying to make my works to act as a barrier for such kind of in humanitarian acts that should never enter in the coming next century so that the next coming 30th century can be called as refined.

Hari Das

I was Written in Streets so don't send me back there again if you liked it pass it away to someone else in Need.

If liked my work mail me at haridaswrites@yahoo.in

To Be Continued

An Ink Fruit

Streets (VOLUME II)

Mumbai

Hari Das